Liam

January 2007

In the same collection,

Lucien Bély

MONT SAINT-MICHEL FOR YOUNG PEOPLE

Illustrated by Pierre Joubert
Translated by Paul Williams

« History in Pictures »
a collection edited by Lucien Bély

ÉDITIONS OUEST-FRANCE
13 rue du Breil, Rennes

The story of the rock, the forest and the sea

Try to imagine the Mont Saint-Michel before anything was built on it. It was a two hundred and fifty foot high rock with sheer sides. The granite which it is made up of, is a very hard rock which, for thousands of years, has resisted erosion from wind and water. This is the reason why this rock, together with one or two others, stands out in what is generally low-lying country.

Around the rock there was a thick forest, which may have been called Scissy Forest. It has now disappeared, for the sea over the years engulfed it. Some tree trunks have actually been found buried in the sand. According to legend, an enormous tidal wave swept over the area, transforming it completely at the beginning of the 8th century when Bishop Aubert dedicated the rock to Saint Michael. Ever since then, it has been an island just like the rock next to it, which is known as Tombelaine.

The tide in the bay where the rock stands, is among the strongest in the world. The difference in depth of water between low and high tide in the same place is around forty feet. The beaches are almost completely flat. The sea has to come in many miles in just a few hours before reaching high water mark. The sea comes in at an amazing speed. It can be as fast as a horse at the gallop, and can prove quite dangerous for people fishing or walking on the beach.

Three rivers flow out onto the shore : the Sée, the Sélune and the Couesnon. The latter marks the boundary between Brittany and Normandy, for as the old saying goes : ''The Couesnon's act of folly left the Mont in Normandy''. The grey silt, known locally as ''tangue'', gives delicate colouring to the landscape. Grass grows on those areas of the sandy shore which are no longer covered at high tide. The sheep that graze there, are known locally as ''prés-salés'' (salt-meadow) sheep because of the salty tang in the grass.

In this land of sand, sky and sea was built an abbey in the style of a citadel, the overall height of which, including the church's steeple, is well over five hundred feet.

The hermits

As the Roman Empire declined, a new religion appeared : Christianity. Men who believed in one God and in his son, Jesus of Nazareth, were overrunning Europe. They swept aside Roman gods and the ancient gods who inhabited woods and pools of water. To escape from the company of their fellow men and from worldly pleasures, holy men, called hermits, lived in great poverty in lonely forests and deserted islands. The place which we now call Mont Saint-Michel was known in those days as Mont Tombe which meant literally "tomb on a hill". The rock no doubt attracted hermits, for Christians, perhaps from Ireland, had settled very early on around the bay and near Dol-de-Bretagne. A remarkable legend tells us how fishermen provided food for the hermits living on the Mont. Whenever a hermit went hungry, he lit a fire ; the villagers saw the smoke and loaded up a donkey with provisions. God then guided it through what remained of the Forest of Scissy until it arrived safely at the holy man's refuge. One day a wolf devoured the innocent donkey and, as a punishment, God forced it to carry all the provisions from then on.

Meanwhile, the cult of Saint Michael was spreading from the East towards Gaul. Heavenly beings were associated with Christ. Among them were the angels and the archangels Michael, Raphael and Gabriel. According to the Bible, when Lucifer, the fallen angel, compared himself with God, another angel stood up before him and shouted "Who is like God ?", in other words Mi-ka-el, or Michael.

God entrusted him to lead his army, for Michael is "Prince of the Heavenly Host". He wears a suit of armour or a long white tunic. He holds a sparkling sword or lance. In the *Apocalypse,* a book written by the Apostle, Saint John, a dragon with seven crowned heads and ten horns, and a tail that swept aside the stars, threatened the Virgin Mary and her Holy Child who had just been born. Michael and his angels fought this serpent from Satan and destroyed it.

The town of Avranches, which is very close to the Mont, in the year 708 was ruled by a bishop called Aubert. One night, he saw Saint Michael in a dream. The Archangel ordered him to make the rock that had just been surrounded by the sea, into a place of worship dedicated to him. Aubert did nothing about it, thinking his imagination had got the better of him. Saint Michael grew impatient with him, and when he appeared the third time, he poked a hole in Aubert's skull to make him believe. He caused many more miracles to take place, so as to convince the bishop and his followers. A bull that had been stolen, was found at the very top of the Mont, as Michael had predicted. One story

Aubert dedicates the rock to Saint Michael

The Archangel often appeared in Italy : in Rome near the castle which still bears the name Holy Angel, and at Monte Gargano, a rocky peninsular on the Adriatic Sea.

has it that Aubert was to build his church as large as the area trodden on by the bull ; according to another story, it was to occupy the space left dry in the midst of the morning dew.

Aubert fulfilled Michael's wishes and despatched messengers to Monte Gargano in Italy. They brought back some sacred relics : a piece of the red cloak worn by the Archangel during one of his apparitions, and a fragment of the altar where he had placed his foot.

When they returned, Aubert began to construct the sanctuary.

The builders received some divine assistance with their task. An old man who lived nearby was called by God to move a huge stone. Another story tells of how a small child simply touched it with his foot and pushed it over the edge. There was no drinking water on the rock, but miraculously a spring was discovered. This is now called Saint Aubert's spring.

As time went by, the rock began to be known as Mont Saint-Michel, and Aubert sent a few men to live there and pray to God and his Archangel.

The foundation of the abbey

The peace and prosperity brought by Charlemagne lasted a short while. Men from the North, or Normans, came and pillaged the coast every year. Their fast, slender boats, known as drakkars, brought widespread terror. Above all else, they pillaged sanctuaries where there were objects of gold for the glory of God. The Mont had its fair share of these dreadful expeditions. In the end, the Normans came and settled, and the king of the Franks recognised one of their chiefs, Rolf le Marcheur, or Rollon, as the "Duke of Normandy". In exchange, the formidable warrior became a Christian along with all his soldiers, and from then on protected all those in God's service.

Rollon and his descendants encouraged the rebuilding of important sanctuaries. But these new converts to the faith had high standards. Duke Richard reproached the priests who lived on the Mont for their immoral and impious behaviour. He threw them out

12

and replaced them in 966 with submissive and humble monks from Flanders guided by a man of noble family called Maynard. These eleven monks adopted the rule of Saint Benedict which required them to organise their lives according to the principles of poverty, chastity and obedience. The abbey had become a Benedictine abbey.

The monk's leader was the abbot, or "father" of the community. He administered all the possessions of the monastery, encouraged the cult of Saint Michael, and received visitors. Theoretically, the monks themselves elected their own superior, but in practice, the Duke of Normandy, as protector of the abbey, persisted in selecting his own candidate for a long time.

This gave rise to many disputes and conflicts. However, certain abbots won universal admiration through their faith, authority and generosity. Bernard du Bec, for example, in the 12th century, made bad monks go and live solitary lives on Tombelaine Island ; he excommunicated a nobleman for thieving ; he had a Benedictine habit taken to a sick knight on his deathbed. In this way, he brought more prestige and power to the abbey.

13

The romanesque age

The monks' vocation was to pray, both for themselves and for all men. Behind the high walls of the monastery, in the "enclosure", they avoided, as far as they could, all worldly temptations and violence. Their day was divided into eight hours : Matins at daybreak, Lauds, Prime, Terce, Sext around midday, Nones, Vespers, and Compline at the end of the day. Each of these hours was accompanied by prayers which were read out of "books of hours", or breviaries.

Knights, in feudal times, engaged themselves in the profession of arms. But as death grew near, they turned to the abbeys. A captain, Néel de Saint-Sauveur, sought refuge and peace on the Mont Saint-Michel. Many warriors too asked to be buried in holy ground near sanctuaries.

When the old buildings were no longer big enough, the abbey, because of its wealth, was able to expand. An immense church was built at the top of the rock, to serve as a grandiose setting for prayer. Building techniques had progressed in Normandy. The style of architecture that later came

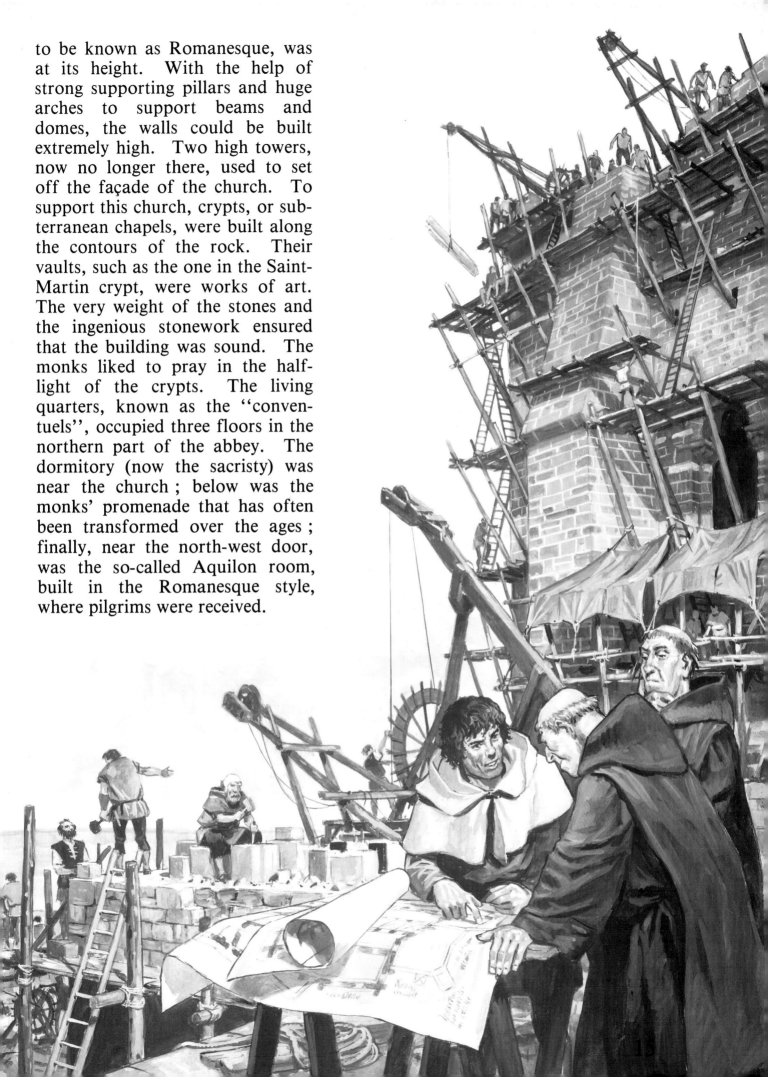

to be known as Romanesque, was at its height. With the help of strong supporting pillars and huge arches to support beams and domes, the walls could be built extremely high. Two high towers, now no longer there, used to set off the façade of the church. To support this church, crypts, or sub-terranean chapels, were built along the contours of the rock. Their vaults, such as the one in the Saint-Martin crypt, were works of art. The very weight of the stones and the ingenious stonework ensured that the building was sound. The monks liked to pray in the half-light of the crypts. The living quarters, known as the ''conven-tuels'', occupied three floors in the northern part of the abbey. The dormitory (now the sacristy) was near the church ; below was the monks' promenade that has often been transformed over the ages ; finally, near the north-west door, was the so-called Aquilon room, built in the Romanesque style, where pilgrims were received.

Famous pilgrims

Very soon, famous pilgrims came to the Mont Saint-Michel to implore the Archangel's protection. Richard II, Duke of Normandy, married Judith of Brittany there in the presence of the nobility of both provinces. On that occasion, he offered the abbey some churches, mills, lands and forests. One Duke of Brittany placed on the altar, property deeds of lands which he was making over to the monastery. These numerous gifts amounted to a vast amount of property all around the Bay. Peasants, that worked on these lands, regularly transported to the island, either by boat or on carts at low tide, part of their harvests. In exchange they received protection and justice.

The abbot, in his turn, honoured the protectors of the abbey. When Duke William completed the conquest of England, the superior of the Mont sent six ships and four monks to salute the new king. The finest of all the abbots was Robert de Thorigny who had been a skilful member of the Court of the Plantagenet King, Henry II, who reigned over England and a large part of France. This abbot administered the abbey at the peak of its fortune.

He welcomed there a whole line of magnificent princes. King Henry II, whom he served as counsellor, came and visited him, accompanied by King Louis VII of France, the Archbishop of Rouen,

two cardinals who later became Popes, and five abbots. Their entrance into the abbey was an occasion for sumptuous ceremony. The entire community awaited the royal visitors on the shore at the entrance to the town with the Gospels, incense and holy water. All the bells rang out as the distinguished gathering made for the church.

Robert de Thorigny added to the community by recruiting a larger number of monks during his travels ; he enriched the library, and finally had built, on the south-west side of the abbey, a huge hostel for pilgrims, which collapsed at the beginning of the 19th century. On the west side, he built his own quarters.

The miracles

Whenever some strange, fortuitous event occurred on the Mont, it was always attributed to the influence of Saint Michael. The monks built up a whole collection of these "miracles" which pilgrims and travellers passed down over the centuries.

One day, a blind woman stood in front of the Mont, and when her face turned towards it, she recovered her sight. "How beautiful it is to be able to see", she exclaimed and the name Beauvoir (beautiful to see) was given to the village where she was. Another woman, who was expecting a child, unwisely attempted to cross the shore. She suddenly felt the first birth pangs and fell to the sand. The tide was

coming in, but a miracle took place and she was spared. When the fishermen found her safe and sound, her child had been born. A cross, the Croix des Grèves (shore cross), was erected to mark the spot where it had happened. It stayed there for many centuries before being engulfed by the waves.

The men of the Middle Ages thought that the bones of saints had miraculous powers. The bones of Bishop Aubert, now Saint Aubert, had disappeared. A long time after the foundation of the abbey, a piece of music, that the monks thought had been sent from heaven, began to be heard. They started to look for it and questioned the nephew of one of the canons who had previously been expelled. At last, some chests were found hidden in the dormitory ceiling. A miraculous force caused the locks to open and inside were the Saint's relics. A parchment was found, that proved the authenticity of the bones. Hence, for centuries, pilgrims stood in awe before a skull with a hole in it, the one that Saint Michael had made in Aubert's forehead.

Religious feasts

The men of the Middle Ages liked religious feasts. The architecture of the Mont, with its huge church, mysterious crypts and great stairways, lent itself well to splendid ceremonies.

There were frequent processions through the abbey. The abbot then, just like a bishop, wore a mitre and carried a crook. The monks, instead of their severe, rough habits, wore copes (sleeveless cloaks), or white habits known as albs. The whole monastery was lit up with candles. The relics in their reliquaries, and the Gospels, were taken among the pilgrims in the midst of clouds of incense. The procession came to a halt at special places where fervent prayers were said.

These ceremonies could turn into veritable theatrical shows. Monks

played the parts of characters in the New Testament to help everyone understand the sacred texts, in the style of mystery plays held in front of cathedrals. In the 12th century, a monk from the Mont, who was a poet, wrote in the vernacular which all could understand (and not in Latin which was the language of the church), some verses which told the abbey's history and the miracles which had been wrought there. It was called the *Roman du Mont Saint-Michel* (The story of the Mont Saint-Michel) and was the work of a monk who had all the qualities of a real minstrel.

These ceremonies were always accompanied by singing, the monks' one passion. The human voice enhanced prayer. This plain song, or Gregorian chant, by virtue of its austerity and simplicity, was a form of worship in itself.

Finally, the reception of a new monk involved a moving ceremony. The young man's head was partly shaved : this was called the "tonsure", and was a symbol of his ecclesiastical calling. After one year's observation, he was allowed to take his vows in front of the whole community. The abbot helped him to put on a monk's habit to the accompaniment of songs of praise, and bestowed upon him a kiss of peace. For three days, he then prayed in the church. But after that, he was judged worthy to be a monk.

The marvel

At the beginning of the 13th century, the great Anglo-Norman kingdom broke up. The King of France, Philippe-Auguste, took Normandy after a number of bloody battles. In the meantime, Mont Saint-Michel was besieged by an ally of the French King. The town and the abbey were in part destroyed by fire. In order to be pardoned and to convert the monastery to his cause, Philippe-Auguste sent a large amount of gold there, for it was necessary to rebuild.

A new art form, known later as "Gothic", was beginning to gain a hold. It was the age of the cathedral. The "ogival" arch led to the construction of particularly spacious and high buildings. The abbots of the Mont and their architects concentrated on the monk's living quarters. This was how the "Merveille", or "Marvel", came to be built on the north side. It was a masterpiece of Gothic architecture. The Romanesque buildings were no longer large enough to accommodate the monks, whose numbers had increased, for they too were changing with the times and were con-

22

tide from the Chausey Islands off the Mont. Stonemasons carved the granite into the correct shape. Sometimes they decorated it. Then with the help of ropes, pulleys or hoists such as the one that can still be seen at the Mont, the materials were hoisted up the scaffolding. When everything was assembled, the wooden supporting frames were removed.

cerned with more comfort and beauty to suit their life style.

The architects were certainly ambitious to dare to build such a high and vast building on this steep rock. Enormous buttresses were built on the outside to shore up the Marvel. But, at the same time, as the construction got higher, it had to become less and less massive, so as to forestall any possibility of collapse — a not infrequent occurrence in the history of the Mont. The almonry and the store house on the bottom floor had very thick walls and strong vaults ; on the second floor, the Guests' room and the Knights' room had columns and ogival arches to support the third floor which contained the refectory and the cloister.

The stones arrived by sea at high

The life of the monks

From now on, the monks spent most of their time in the Marvel. Poor pilgrims were welcomed in the almonry, rich ones on the floor above, in the Guests' room. Both places were near the entrance which, like it is today, was to the east, and not to the north-west as in the Romanesque era. The community kept well out of the way on the higher floors of the Marvel, near the church.

The thick walls of the refectory were pierced with long narrow windows that let in plenty of light, and supported a fine wooden "cradle" vault. Meals took place in silence while one monk read sacred texts from a pulpit situated on the south wall. The cloister, suspended in mid-air between sea and sky, was for taking a stroll, for meditation and conversation. The arcades are supported on fine columns of purple stone. Above the columns, the soft, white limestone of Caen has been carved into flowers and leaves. These carvings are an admirable example of Norman decorative art.

Before the introduction of printing, the only way of preserving and reproducing a text was to copy it by hand. This was done by the monks, who went to great pains to decorate and beautify manuscripts. This was the art of illumination. Colours and designs were used to illuminate and illustrate individual letters. The Mont was known as the "city of books", for there were so many fine works in its library. The monks were not only interested in sacred texts and prayers, but also the works of Antiquity. The "chauffoir", or hot room, was the place where the monks conducted this meticulous work, as well as everything else. This room, that was later called the " Knights' " room, shows only too well that the monks' main enemy was the dank cold that came from the sea and the mist. They fought against it by lighting huge fires, and using tapestries and furs for insulation. Indeed, many monks preferred to live inland, in priories under the control of the abbey.

Pilgrimages

In the Middle Ages, it was considered a duty to go on a pilgrimage. The richest or the bravest went to the Holy Land, Rome or Compostella. Others had to be content with a sanctuary that was nearer home. The Mont Saint-Michel, of course, was a great Norman centre of pilgrimage, but it also attracted pilgrims from all over France and all of western Christendom. Christians went there to pray to the Archangel for their sins to be forgiven and for all their hopes to come true. Ill people especially hoped that a miracle would give them back their health, as used to happen in the legends emanating from the Mont.

Sometimes God's calling was sudden and inexplicable : a man could set off for the Mont in the middle of shoeing a horse, leaving the job unfinished. In 1333, the entire population of a village suddenly left for the Mont, forcing their parish priest to go with them and say Mass there.

A pilgrim on his way to the Mont was called a "miquelot". Like all other pilgrims, he was recognisable by his leather sack that was carried over his right shoulder, and by his roughly hewn staff. He would also have shells, the very symbols of a pilgrimage, stitched to his clothing. A pilgrim could expect help and respect on his journey. He was given shelter for the night in special inns right the way along the roads leading to the Mont. These roads were called "the ways of Paradise".

He was threatened by many a danger, among them illness and fatigue. When he finally caught sight of the famous shape of the Mont he shouted out "Mont-joie", Mount Joy, in his great relief. Even then, he still had two or three kilometres to go, across the shore where quicksands and the rising tide were still dangers to be reckoned with. Tramps could also mislead pilgrims in the mist and then steal their money.

ed to repeat the experience of Norgod, Bishop of Avranches, who saw a bright light come down to the rock thereby revealing the presence of Saint Michael. Others even tried to spend the night in the dark church, only to give up after one of them was slapped by the invisible hand of God.

The pilgrim took part in the religious festivals. He tried to touch the reliquaries which contained the precious relics, the most curious of which were a tiny sword and shield that the archangel is said to have used to kill a dragon, and that had been brought by some miraculous means from a far-off country. The faithful pilgrim was also expected to make offerings : King Philip the Fair gave a statue covered in gold ; the poor made do with a piece of wax that went towards lighting the chapels.

Miquelots at the mont

All kinds came to the Mont : invalids, pilgrims and wrong-doers mixed together, and all languages and dialects could be heard. Everyone was full of hope. Some want-

The town nestling at the foot of the abbey welcomed the travellers. They dined in the taverns and slept in the hostelries. But important visitors were received by the abbot in the very large and bright Guests' room. Food was prepared in the two enormous hearths that were hidden from the rest of the room by sumptuous tapestries. Lavatories were installed in the north wall. The reception room with its elegant columns was richly adorned. Beneath it, however, near the entrance to the Gothic abbey, was the simple and austere almonry where the poorest people could get food.

In the town, shops sold special pilgrim souvenirs known as "enseignes", or signs. These were little silver or metal brooches representing Saint Michael or the outline of a shell, though some pilgrims were quite content to take home a cockle-shell picked up on the shore.

The abbey and the one hundred years' war

War broke out at the beginning of the 14th century between France and England, and took its toll together with the plague, which was then spreading throughout the whole of Christendom. It came to be called the "One Hundred Years' War".

After the serious French defeats at Poitiers and Crécy, King Charles V began to make a comeback with the help of his constable, Bertrand Duguesclin. This Breton knight was the captain of the Mont Saint-Michel. When he left France for Spain, he entrusted his wife, Tiphaine Raguenel, to the protection of Saint Michael the Archangel. She lived in a house built at the top of the town, undertaking good works and practising the science of astrology which she was devoted to : she could read the future of the world in the movement of the stars.

On the occasion of one of his visits to the abbey, the mad King, Charles VI, made the abbot Pierre le Roi, who was an academic of some standing, into his counsellor. He immediately began to fortify the abbey. He defended the entrance by building towers, successive courtyards, and ramparts, thereby creating a veritable fort together with its "barbican". He completed the living quarters on the south side. These were reserved for the abbot and for the administrative and judiciary offices.

Normandy fell into English hands in 1415, after the French defeat at Agincourt. The province was then governed by the Duke of Bedford, the brother of the English King, who succeeded in winning over to his cause a number of leading Norman personalities. Among them was the abbot of the Mont, Robert Jolivet, Pierre le Roi's suc-

cessor, who accepted to be counsellor to Bedford, and received, in exchange, all the property belonging to the monastery.

The monks refused to support their treacherous abbot. Some knights, who had been dispossessed of their lands, had sought refuge with them, and they stayed faithful to the French cause, the only defender of which was the Dauphin Charles, who was later to become Charles VII, the so-called "King of Bourges".

The Romanesque chancel at the Mont collapsed and, because of the war, it was impossible to reconstruct it. One of the Mont's captains died in combat ; the small island of Tombelaine fell into English hands ; and, as a sinister omen of things to come, the river Couesnon changed course after an unusually high tide.

31

The shepherd lads and lasses

During these troubled times in the first half of the XIVth century, a strange phenomenon occurred. Despite all the dangers involved, children began to go on pilgrimage to the Mont Saint-Michel. They were called the "shepherd lads and lasses" in popular ballads and tales. A chronicle from the town of Cologne in Germany contains a description of these great child crusades : "That year, there was a great pilgrimage to the Mont Saint-Michel in Normandy, a pilgrimage that lasted about two years and which was made up of small children of eight, nine, ten and twelve years of age, that came from all the towns and villages of Germany and Belgium, and other countries too. They gathered together in large numbers, abandoning their parents, and marched along, two by two, in procession. At the head of the column were students bearing effigies of Saint Michael. Children from the same area group-

ed together behind their own standard, which was decorated with the coats of arms of their local gentry. These children inspired pity, for they had left their homes against the wishes of their parents and without any money for the journey. Nevertheless, they remained in good health, for all along the road they were given food and drink in sufficient quantities. When they arrived at the Mont Saint-Michel, they offered their standards to the Archangel. On the way there, the procession attracted old people, valets and servants of both sexes..." These rowdy, undisciplined crowds of people shocked their contempo-

raries, for they were made up of children who had no hesitation in abandoning family, town and country. But such pilgrimages also worried the grave fathers of the Church who saw in them a source of disorder and unrest.

We know they lasted for a long time, for an 18th century man of letters, Rétif de la Bretonne, quotes a popular ditty of the time :

"Little Jack is on a pilgrimage
to Saint Michael,
may he be guided on his way
by Raphael.
Here we used to watch over
the white sheep together.
Little Jack crosses over the
                    [shaking bridge
in search of a pardon"

The siege of the mont

The beginning of the XVth. century was a critical period for the Mont Saint-Michel.

The English decided to storm this stronghold which dared to stand up to them. A citadel that was defended both by its ramparts and by the sea was impregnable. It had to be surrounded and obliged to give itself up through famine and lack of water.

The siege began in 1424. Numerous troops took up positions around the Bay. A small wooden fort called the "bastille" was constructed at Ardevon, in front of the Mont, as a refuge in the event of an attack, and in order to keep a watch over the shore. Finally, a flotilla arrived to complete the blockade, from the sea.

Some Breton noblemen com-manded an expedition from Saint-Malo and skilfully attacked the English ships and managed to disperse them. This naval victory enabled the Mont to receive provisions by sea. The siege had failed utterly and the citadel had not surrendered.

For the first time in a long while, the French were able to recover their confidence. It seemed that the Archangel himself had made this victory possible, and his cult won all the more prestige. This is why Saint Michael was among those who appeared to Joan of Arc. He told her : "I am Michael, the protector of France. Arise, and go to help the King of France". And he guided the shepherd girl from Lorraine through her great adventures.

Charles VII put a very able captain, called Louis d'Estouteville,

34

in charge of the Mont's garrison. He set about putting an end to the squabbles, schemings, pillaging and debauchery that were now common in the abbey, and had been introduced by rough, coarse soldiers who knew no better. Because he tightened up discipline in this way, the citadel was able to withstand the last attack by the English in 1433. A fire broke out in the town, destroying the wooden houses and damaging the ramparts. The English tried to take advantage of this by coming in large numbers with terrible war engines which succeeded in breaching the walls. For a while, they thought they had taken the town, but the garrison held on, and, in the end, the English were forced to withdraw. The shore was strewn with the dead, and the knights from the Mont retrieved two enormous cannons which were set up at the entrance to the town where they can still be seen.

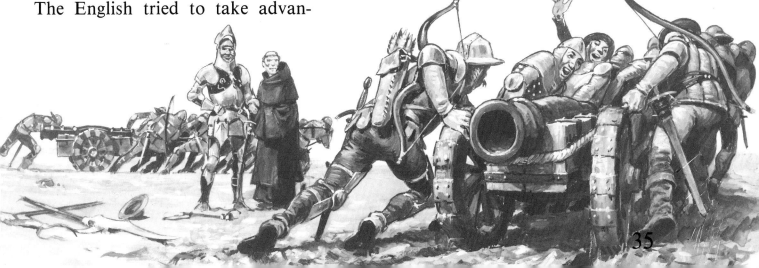

The knights of Saint Michael

The King at the end of the Middle Ages, Louis XI, was an able but cruel monarch. He was very devout, and even superstitious. He loved pilgrimages, which is why he twice visited the sanctuary which symbolised the French victory over the English.

It was this that made him think of creating the Order of the Knights of Saint Michael, with the Archangel as its first member. The Duke of Burgundy, who was a great enemy of the King, already had the Knights of the Golden Fleece. But the Knights of Saint Michael were the King's own creation and were chosen from among the finest noblemen of the kingdom. They received a necklace of golden shells on which hung a medal which depicted Michael slaying the dragon, and had written on it the motto of the Order : "Immensi terror oceani" (the terror of the immense ocean).

The dignitaries wore white damask robes and a red velvet head-dress. They took part in splendid ceremonies presided over by the King at the chapel of Saint Michael in the heart of Paris.

The King had another idea which was nothing short of lugubrious. He ordered a wood and metal cage to be suspended from the ceiling at the Mont. Every time the prisoner inside moved, the whole contraption began to rock. Being in this confined space in the freezing and lonely old abbey, was just like being in Hell. For centuries, political prisoners who had offended the King or his servants, were locked away there. Some were left for years at the mercy of the rats ; some ended up going mad.

The last constructions

Captain d'Estouteville had strengthened the abbey's defences. The town, which had always been threatened in war, had been encircled by ramparts and strong towers such as the Roy, Cholet, Beatrix and Arcade towers. With all its cannons, machicolations through which various objects could be dropped in defence, and watch-towers which commanded a view over the shores, the Mont Saint-Michel had become one of the strongest forts of its day. A lot of progress had been made during the long war in the art of attack and self-defence.

Abbot Jolivet had died at Rouen in the midst of the English whom he had served well. Louis d'Estouteville had appointed his brother, Guillaume, as abbot of the Mont. This man was a prince of the Church, a cardinal. He wasn't a monk but a priest. His many important commitments prevented him from devoting all his time to the monastery, which he left in the hands of the prior. Thus started the "commendam" system, which

involved the abbot residing outside his community while receiving the greater part of their revenue. From that time on, the King handed over numerous abbeys to important people whom he wanted to honour or reward.

The cardinal's prestige and his influence with the Pope and the King speeded up the reconstruction of the church. A crypt, known as "the crypt of the wide pillars", supported the new construction which was finished at the beginning of the 16th century. The tall, graceful chancel is lit by high windows, and a gallery with delicate carvings and tracery. To support the building at the top of the rock, flying buttresses were positioned to act as props. The outside was finished off with "pinnacles", or fine pyramids decorated with flowers. Because of its rich profusion of detail, this style was known as the "flamboyant" style. A "lacework stairway" (the name is well chosen) gives access through this forest of granite right up to the roof, from where the whole sweep of the Bay can be seen.

The wars of religion

At the beginning of the 16th. century, one of the King's lieutenants completed the defences of the town. From now on, the entrance to the town was well protected by the Avancée, Boulevard and Roy gates, which were reinforced by the addition of a moat, drawbridge and portcullis.

Throughout the century, the Kings of France visited the famous abbey, and François 1st. was received there with great pomp. But the wars of religion threw the kingdom into confusion, and the Mont was caught up in a whirlwind of battles and massacres.

The Protestants tried to capture this Catholic stronghold. Since it was reputed to be impregnable, Captain Le Touchet endeavoured, in 1577, to take it through cunning. Men disguised as pilgrims hid their weapons and managed to get within

the walls. They won over the soldiers watching the abbey gates by offering them wine, and then took up their positions on the Saut-Gauthier to await reinforcements. A novice (future monk) from the abbey realised what they were up to and gave the alarm. The monks alerted the townspeople at the foot of the monastery. When they realised they had been discovered, the false pilgrims tried to bluff their way out by shouting "the town has been taken", but the inhabitants took up their arms to help the monks. Captain Le Touchet, who was just arriving with his horsemen, had to turn back, leaving his companions to surrender.

Another stratagem was used later by members of the formidable Montgomery family. Men disguised as women and fishermen approached the Mont. The guards at the town gate grew suspicious and killed them all in cold blood. The Huguenot troops appeared

from nowhere and took the town. But the abbey continued to resist. The military governor was away from the Mont at the time, but as soon as he received news of what was happening, he gathered some men and rushed back. They hoisted themselves up, with the help of ropes, to the ramparts above the occupied town and started a counter-offensive. The Protestants, caught between two lines of fire, were defeated, and all the prisoners were locked up on Tombelaine Island.

The abbey in ruins

Monastic life was on the wane. The monks began to abandon their abbey : some of them preferred to live in the taverns. They were no longer respected. The abbots, such as Abbot de Guise or Cardinal de Montmorency, were selected by the King from amongst the finest nobility. But they no longer visited the Mont : they were quite content to collect some of its revenue. An unexpected revival took place when new Benedictines, the Maurists, took it over. These learned men were devoted to the history of the Mont, which they studied from the collection of manuscripts that had been built up over the ages.

The buildings were badly maintained and virtually falling into ruin. Both the high towers and three supporting arches in the church collapsed. They were not rebuilt in their original style but replaced in 1780 by a very simple classical façade.

Meanwhile, the abbey was transformed into a prison and became the "sea Bastille". Writs were issued by the King to banish to the island without fair trial, debauched aristocrats, corrupt priests and

political opponents. The worst of them were shut up in dank, dark dungeons, or, indeed, in Louis XI's famous cage.

In 1788, the sons of the Duke of Orleans visited the Mont Saint-Michel guided by their governess, Madame de Genlis, a famous novelist and educator. In 1830, the eldest, Philippe, became King Louis-Philippe 1st. During dinner, the prisoners were brought in and they told of their extraordinary adventures. The following day, the young princes visited the crypts and the dungeons. They saw the cage, "that monument of barbarism", were told its history, and promptly asked for it to be done away with. A Swiss soldier who earned money by showing it to visitors, received a tidy sum in compensation. The door of the cage was taken off in the presence of the children.

Louis-Philippe was then seventeen years of age. We can just imagine his younger brother, the little Count of Beaujolais, being determined to do away with such a frightful contraption.

The resurrection of the Mont

The French Revolution got rid of the last of the monks but the Mont Saint-Michel continued to be a prison. From now on, the whole abbey was a dark and terrible prison. Each riot or failed uprising brought a new batch of political prisoners. Victor Hugo evoked the tragic fate of those men : "All around us, as far as the eye can see, infinite space, the blue horizon of the sea, the green horizon of the land, clouds, air, liberty, birds wheeling, ships at full sail ; and then suddenly, over the top of the old wall above our heads, the pale face of a prisoner".

Some, like Colombat the painter, managed to escape. He got hold of an old nail after a fire in the abbey and made a hole in the wall.

An accomplice got some rope to him, hidden in a loaf of bread. While the watch was changing, he let himself down the high wall. He was safe, and his escape made him famous overnight. Another famous prisoner, Barbès, tried to imitate him but, buffetted by the wind and blinded by the fog, he let go the rope and ended up with a broken leg. The garrison was alerted and he was recaptured.

The abbey was rediscovered by visitors and Romantic writers during the 19th century. They admired the extraordinary architecture. This was the birth of tourism. The prison was abolished under the Second Empire. In 1874, the Mont had become a "historic monument".

The Mont Saint-Michel rose again from its ruins. Restoration

44

was undertaken, with extreme attention to detail. The Gothic steeple was rebuilt, thus giving the finishing touch to the famous silhouette rising above the sand. A single monk, and then a little community, came and revived the religious tradition. This abbey, which is also a citadel, bears witness to one thousand years of effort to please God, monks and pilgrims alike.